Sylvia J Adams

DO YOUR MARRIAGE GOOD

HOW TO LOVE AND REGARD YOUR SPOUSE

INTRODUCTION

With regards to relationships, regard between companions is an unquestionable necessity for a blissful and satisfied relationship, and the subject of how to regard your better half more isn't unreasonably usually inquired.

Nonetheless, it ought to stand out than it is.

Here is the reason: the two mates ought to similarly regard each other since, in such a case that you need regard, you're probably going to slip into brutal contentions, battles and you are bound to utilize destructive words.

Instructions to Regard Your Companion

For what reason would it be a good idea for you to regard your significant other?

Over and over again, we disregard the "more grounded sex" in the relationship and marriage, and we misjudge the significance of showing them the amount we regard them.

Anyway, for what reason is your regard essential to your significant other?

At the point when you show your better half the amount you value him and regard what he does or thinks, you're charging his batteries, and he is prepared to vanquish the world realizing he has you close by. It resembles you're giving him the wings to would whatever both of you like to do.

It is an indication that you trust him. "Regard won't exist except if trust exists first," and it's the essential fact of the matter.

You are likewise recognizing him as a decent pioneer who is equipped for dealing with his loved ones.

In addition, regard likewise gives consolation to improve and, surprisingly, harder things. In any event, when he feels crushed, your little uplifting statements will go quite far to move him along.

Chapter 1

20 methods for showing your significant other Love

To know how to regard your better half somewhat more and how to recognize your significant other, read on and learn straightforward things that can work on your relationship.

1. Really focus on him

Time after time, we're occupied by gadgets or different things when our companions are conversing with us. Some stare at the television, others shop on the web or peruse virtual entertainment.

Things being what they are, how could a spouse regard her better half?

Assuming that he's addressing you, quit all that you're doing and look at him without flinching when you both are imparting. Assuming you're figuring how to regard your significant other and how to recognize your better half, we have extraordinary news - it's these little things!

2. Get some information about his day and show certified interest

Dark Sweetheart Giving Beau Back rub At Home

Basic inquiries like "How was your day" can mean a ton and is an extraordinary method for recognizing your better half.

You need to show authentic interest in his exercises and, in particular, his sentiments and contemplations about whatever occurred during the day. This will assist you with understanding what he's going through, and you can

3. Ask him how he feels

Folks can be exceptionally hesitant, and they attempt to put a fearless face on imagining that uncovering their actual sentiments implies they are powerless.

Tell him he can impart everything to you. Spouses ought to regard husbands since it can either make them or break them. Tell him you're his protected zone and that you love him and regard him, regardless of his shortcomings.

4. Grin more regularly

Grin is a widespread language of joy. Send a few joy your significant other's way and show the adoration for your better half with this basic yet significant motion.

Numerous ladies say, "I have my own particular manners of cherishing my significant other," yet everybody feels much improved when they see a grin on their darling one's face, so be liberal with grins and kind words.

. Allow him to be the chief (every so often ▯)

Most men need consolation that they are sufficient, sufficient, adequately brilliant.

Recognize your better half by allowing him to choose where you'll go for supper or what film you'll watch. Perhaps you're not 100 percent in Quick and Enraged, yet assuming that this will fulfill him, share this involvement in him, he will see the value in it.

A similar applies to sexual coexistence. Permit him to communicate his cravings and dreams, start to lead the pack, and do everything you possibly can for cause him to feel wanted as well.

. Kiss him frequently

Couple Hello Each Other Before She Leaves

We as a whole kiss toward the beginning of connections, yet it's practically similar to life becomes excessively occupied for us. At any rate, you can pause and give each other even a peck on the lips. Snatch him and give him the awesome stomach bending French kiss!

This will deliver chemicals in both of you, and you will in a split second feel more joyful!

7. Ask him for his perspective

Notwithstanding in the event that it's about significant choices or little, get some information about it and pay attention to him eagerly.

You don't have to get a cerebral pain contemplating how to regard your better half. Simply do what you could like him to do, and you'd like him to get some information about your viewpoint, correct?

8. Energize him more

When did you last let him know he's working effectively? Men should be continually reminded (ladies as well!) pretty much every one of the astonishing things they do.

Regarding your man is showing him that you value all that he does, yet in addition letting him know this frequently and assisting him with having more certainty and confidence in himself.

9. Treat him well

Nothing more awful than seeing mates poking fun at their "critical" ones!

On the off chance that there is embarrassment, there is no space for affection here. To extend regard and love, you need to encourage him notwithstanding assuming you're separated from everyone else at home or with companions. Express kind things about him, and you'll see his chest siphoning from affection and pride.

10. Cook for him

Men love home-prepared food. For their purposes, cooking is an approach to showing adoration and commitment to him and the family.

Assuming you're pondering how to regard your significant other more, simply cook him his #1 feast and shock him with heavenly food. "Love gets through the stomach" is an old and exceptionally famous expressing, and there's a valid justification for it.

11. Try not to bother

Nobody likes to pay attention to irritating, particularly not your better half, who just got back home from an unrelenting workday.

Recognize your better half by making it about him, not about you or others, or little things that didn't go how you would have preferred them to go.

At the point when you bother, you channel his energy, and yours as well. Rather than whining about things, attempt to really impact point of view and be appreciative for everything great that happened that day. This will help both of you feel more joyful and feeling better.

12. Concede when you're off-base

How to regard your significant other in the event that you have quite recently had a battle and you can't deal with it?

Furthermore, you realize it was your issue, all things considered, then, at that point, apologize.

Try not to allow senseless pride to negatively affect your relationship with him. "I'm grieved" can be the enchanted word, and it will assist him with feeling your regard for him as well, by showing you see him as equivalent and that you love him enough to put his sentiments over your pride.

13. Set aside a few minutes for you two

Regarding your man implies ensuring both of you actually possess energy for one another. An odd date, or a walk around the recreation area, in any case, that an Unquestionable requirement assuming you believe your marriage should endure.

14. Wear his #1 outfit and hurl on some make

Men (and ladies as well) love seeing wonderful things, whether it's scene, painting, or a beautiful face. You can shock your man by putting on a touch of cosmetics and wearing a pleasant outfit (or purchasing a decent arrangement of undergarments), regardless of whether it's daily you're spending together.

What should be done for your significant other don't need to cost a great deal or take a ton of time. They can be simply insightful shocks like this.

15. Express gratitude toward him

There are 1,000,000 different ways on the best way to regard your significant other more, and one of them is just saying thanks to him more regularly. "Much thanks to you" is a particularly straightforward expression, however it means everything to individuals who hear it.

Let's assume it with certified care and a heart loaded with sympathy and understanding.

He will adore you much more, realizing you value all that he accomplishes for you, even the littlest things, and by knowing this, he will be quicker on doing the greater things for you as well.

16. Support his thoughts

An extraordinary method for recognizing your better half is to help his thoughts. Whether they are business or individual, simply the reality he is imparting them to you ought to be a legitimately big deal to you.

Show him regard and love by supporting him and assisting him with fostering the thoughts further. Nothing can stop a couple who are pulling for one another and rousing each other en route!

7. Acknowledge him as he is

Nobody is great. We as a whole have imperfections and excellencies, yet you will extend regard and love to your better half by tolerating him as he is and by doing whatever it takes not to transform him.

He is making an honest effort, and assuming that you energize him and show him support, significantly more, he will get endlessly better at all that he does. Couples get together in light of the fact that all they see are temperances, yet they stay together on the grounds that they figure out how to adore and acknowledge their imperfections as well.

8. Recognize him as a parent

There are various sorts with regards to nurturing. Some are stricter and more focused, while others are milder with kids.

Try not to scrutinize your spouses' choices when before kids, as this will shake his clout in their eyes and will not create as much regard for him in the event that you continue to say how he

isn't correct and how he's bad at nurturing.

19. See him the manner in which you maintain that he should be

Treat him far and away superior to he merits. You can't transform him by letting him know what's up. In any case, assuming you show him love and care and backing, you will urge him to develop and change himself.

Assuming that you're thinking "cherishing my significant other" is hard, reconsider. Love him for the man you maintain that he should be, and you will end up zeroing in on his ethics more frequently than on his imperfections.

20. Be there when he fizzles and falls

Permitting him to come up short is really great for both of you. Nothing recognizes your better half more than aiding him get up and empowering him to attempt once more. They are noticeably flawed, yet nor are we.

Chapter 2

100 texts to make your wife fall in love all over again

I could do without staying here working when I could be at home doing hot things to you.

For what reason might I at any point lie next to you in bed as opposed to considering/working?

I have an unexpected treat for you sometime in the evening; I believe you will like it!

In the event that I could wear three things of dress or less this evening, what might you decide for me?

I just laid in bed for the last hour contemplating you, think about the thing I was doing!

I cleaned the kitchen today, so I'd have space to have intercourse to you on the table.

Your body looks similarly as in your little dark dress.

I love playing with your hair and your _________

Do you need a back knead, a foot rub, or both?

I'd put on music, yet I would rather not muffle the hints of your attractive little groans.

Try not to stop me once you feel stimulated, on the grounds that I'm anticipating causing you to feel euphoric today.

I can hardly hold back to kiss all aspects of your body.

Do you give it a second thought in the event that my tongue is between your legs when you get up toward the beginning of the day?

Your brain is similarly essentially as attractive as your tight little body.

I can't conclude which portion of your body is more tasty. Give me another taste.

I got a few cuffs and a blindfold. Would it be a good idea for me to put them on you or me?

I heated you some treat, so you can eat it while I eat you.

Would you like to have intercourse in bed or in the shower I just made you?

This evening will be about delight and agony.

I need to hear you taking in my ear when I cause you to feel very great!

This evening you're not permitted to allow your pleasure to top until I say as much.

You won't have the option to move after I'm done with you this evening.

Your heart will beat with complete joy this evening.

I had a hard-on all day since I was unable to quit thinking about that delightful face.

Your snicker turns me on considerably more than your wetness does.

I put your garments in the washer, and presently I will make out with you on top of it.

I've never gotten so horny by simply kissing somebody.

Do you maintain that I should awaken you with breakfast in bed or oral?

I'm so horny pondering seeing you later.

I miss having your arms around me.

I was contemplating you in the shower today!

I miss you overwhelming me.

There is something that makes me insane wet when you are standing directly over me while we're kissing.

I cleaned up the room, yet I don't care either way if you mess up the sheets with me.

I will go down on you, and I won't allow you to contemplate giving back in kind.

I miss having you around me.

I was contemplating you in bed today and saying your name till I hit the large O!

I miss you covering me with joy.

I'm so horny pondering seeing you later.

I will murmur in your ear to make you arrive at the pinnacle of your pleasure while you dig those hot nails into my back!

Regardless of the number of cold showers I that have, I actually can't quit thinking about you.

I know somebody who really likes you...

I revere the sensation of your delicate, plush, and sensitive skin against mine.

I love beginning my day by saying your name without holding back

You look incredible today! Also, how would I be aware? Since you look extraordinary consistently!

ach time I shut my eyes, I see you stripped. However, FYI, I like seeing you stripped with my eyes open ignificantly more!

ello, wild thing… . I was simply pondering you… and all my blood voyaged south.

ou might have a hard time believing what I envisioned the previous evening! I was a fire fighter… and ou were ablaze… fortunately I saved you with my firehose. However, made all of you wet…

simply need to nail you against the wall when you return home! No words! Does that make me a errible man?

understand what you need, however I believe that you should beseech me for it.

ssuming you were here the present moment, I would rip your garments off and toss you onto my bed nd have my direction with you.

ou are certainly the most smoking young lady in this piece of the universe!

o you have any idea that I go through my day pondering you and my late evening dreaming about you?

o many choices… which could you pick? The vehicle? The love seat? The floor? Kitchen table?

This evening I will move slowly and appreciate each bend on your sweet body.

You are sooo substantially more than sex to me... even still... with each astonishing episode, it simply improves.

You weren't given lips like that for anything. Get into high heels, put on some red lipstick, and how about we set out to really utilize them?

The sum of everything on my mind is tasting you over and over and once more...

I was considering getting some delicate rope... would it be advisable for me to get enough for your wrists and lower legs or simply your wrists? All things considered, how about we surrender it to me...

I had the most out of this world fantasy the previous evening... it was about you.

I simply thought about another place that I frantically need to attempt with you.

Could it be said that you are distant from everyone else this evening? Need to play a hot game?

Next time when I'm around you, wear something that keeps me speculating.

I need to be devious with you in the workplace.

I have heard that you shouldn't battle it assuming you like it.

I can't quit glancing through those photos you sent me. You look so attractive.

This evening will be about you, child. Just lay back and unwind.

I miss feeling the bends of your hot body squeezed against mine.

I can hardly stand by to see you so I can run my lips across your lovely neck.

You have no clue about how wonderful you are. A pantheon of Goddesses would begrudge you.

Some way or another you get hotter each damn day.

I never understood what it resembled to severely need somebody this.

I will begin your night with a back rub and end it the manner in which you like to be pleasured the most!

I love the manner in which you contact me. Come over?

You are the hottest lady in any room.

I want to be there with you at this moment. I don't have any idea how much longer I can hold on to see you.

I need to hit your butt, pull your hair, and kiss your neck.

I love the sensation of your skin. It's so delicate and great.

We should carry on one of your dreams this evening.

Your groans are the hottest sound on the planet.

I might run out of coquettish instant messages to ship off you, however my heart won't ever run out of space for you.

Do you like my shirt? It's made of beau material.

Seeing your name on my telephone makes me grin like a moron.

I've needed you from the absolute first second I looked at you.

You are transforming me into a sleep deprived person.

Assuming you realize that my response was "yes," what might you ask me?

I'm so occupied by you, even in my viewpoints. Might you at any point quit being so damn hot briefly?

You're similar to a twister. You simply blow me away!

I'm similar to a Rubik's 3D square. The more you play with me, the harder I get.

I'd walk 1,000 miles just to contact you this evening. Furthermore, 1,000 more assuming that you let me kiss you everywhere.

I've had such countless grimy contemplations about you today. Might you want to hear some of them?

Might it be said that you are depleted? You've been running in my viewpoints the entire day. Bare, more often than not.

In the event that I ate a piece of candy for each second that I considered you, I would have lost every one of my teeth at this point.

I'm sending you to an island brimming with kisses on an ocean of affection!

It's consistently amusing to play with you over texts. Notwithstanding, it makes it challenging for me to incline in and kiss you.

On the off chance that kisses were raindrops, I would send you a flood. You'd require an ark.

You are my heart's incredible experience!

Since I met you, every one of the adoration melodies unexpectedly ended up being about you.

I miss your smell. You smell so lovely!

I miss your provocative suggestive looks. You make me soften and hard simultaneously!